Communism is the virus

The Great Leap Forward in 2020, in Ireland and around the world

Corstown — MMXX

Dedicated to those learning to resist tyranny in the modern world

ISBN: 978-1-71665-362-9

Acknowledgements
I would to thank all who assisted in this research, including the staff at Mullingar and Navan libraries.

CONTENTS

INTRODUCTION

The first question we need to address is the obvious one: is the state's response to the pandemic proportionate and reasonable? Because if so there is no need to delve into any deep criticism or "conspiracy theory" with regard to it.

Mortality rate for Covid-19

Firstly a slight technical note: In studying this you will find references to a CFR and an IFR, the former is the *Case Fatality Rate* which is essentially the number who die as a proportion of those who test positive, and the latter the *Infected Fatality Rate* which attempts to get a complete picture of the proportion of those infected who die, allowing for the fact that the testing criteria might underestimate the degree of infection in the population.

One important study that explains this and attempts to estimate the IFR – which is clearly the most important figure – was prepared by the:

> "The Centre for Evidence-Based Medicine (CEBM) based in the Nuffield Department of Primary Care Health Sciences in the University of Oxford"

which

> "is an academic-led centre dedicated to the practice, teaching and dissemination of high quality evidence-based medicine to improve healthcare in everyday clinical practice"

and

> "there are currently over 25 active staff and honorary members of the CEBM. Many of the active staff include other clinicians, statisticians, epidemiologists, information specialists, quantitative and qualitative researchers."

They say that even for those over 70, without pre-existing

conditions, its likely not to exceed 1% fatality of those infected while for children the rate is in practice zero (which is better even than the annual flu). As regards the overall rate in the general population:

> "Taking account of historical experience, trends in the data, increased number of infections in the population at largest, and potential impact of misclassification of deaths gives a presumed estimate for the COVID-19 IFR somewhere between 0.1% and 0.36%." [1]

Note the decimal point there in case you are not picking up on this properly, the lower band of the estimate gives you a fatality rate, for those who have been infected, of one tenth of one per cent.

Meanwhile another study in April in Santa Clara County, California, by 17 scientists/doctors from Stanford University concluded:

> "A hundred deaths out of 48,000-81,000 infections corresponds to an infection fatality rate of 0.12-0.2%. If antibodies take longer than 3 days to appear, if the average duration from case identification to death is less than 3 weeks, or if the epidemic wave has peaked and growth in deaths is less than 6% daily, then the infection fatality rate would be lower." [2]

To put that in some kind of perspective, the annual flu season fatality rate is about 0.1% while the rate for real genuine health emergency pandemics is a lot different, for example: ebola has a fatality rate of about 50%; the Spanish Flu pandemic had a rate of 2.5%; and the Black Death in the 14th century was estimated to have a mortality rate of about 12.5-66%. In short then, the seriousness of this virus is not even remotely in the category of the great genuine health scares of the past, it is in fact quite logical and reasonable to consider it as nothing more than a bad flu outbreak.

In support of that view we can cite Dr John Ioannidis, inter alia the Professor of Biomedical data science at Stanford University of Medicine and 'one of the most-cited scientists of all times in the scientific literature',[3] who has recently analysed the latest estimates of the IFR for this disease, in particular analysing the 12 big studies which have attempted to arrive at this figure. While three studies are 'modestly higher' and two 'modestly lower' he concluded that:

> "Seven of the 12 inferred IFRs are in the range 0.07 to 0.20 (corrected IFR of 0.06 to 0.16) which are similar to IFR values of seasonal influenza." [4]

Even the go-to US guru on this, Dr Tony Fauci, in his article for the *New England Journal of Medicine* compares Covid-19 to the flu and supports the 0.1% number:

> "This suggests that the overall clinical consequences of Covid-19 may ultimately be more akin to those of a severe seasonal influenza (which has a case fatality rate of approximately 0.1%) or a pandemic influenza (similar to those in 1957 and 1968) rather than a disease similar to SARS or MERS, which have had case fatality rates of 9 to 10% and 36%, respectively." [5]

So there you have it, the best expert voices on this subject are telling you that it is "similar to IFR values of seasonal influenza" and "more akin to those of a severe seasonal influenza...rather than a disease similar to SARS or MERS".

Therefore we can indeed conclude that the state's response to the pandemic is totally disproportionate from what we should expect, and we can move on to ask ourselves why. But before doing so there is one anomaly in the statistics that needs further examination.

Footnotes
1. https://www.cebm.net/covid-19/global-covid-19-case-fatality-rates/ .

2. https://www.medrxiv.org/content/10.1101/2020.03.03.20028423v3.full.pdf .

3. https://prevention.stanford.edu/people/Ioannidis.html .

4.   https://childrenshealthdefense.org/news/lockdown-lunacy-the-thinking-persons-guide/ .

5. https://www.nejm.org/doi/full/10.1056/NEJMe2002387 .

CHAPTER 1
An anomaly in the statistics, why the high death rate in nursing homes?

Hence the pattern of this virus is very clear, it has a 0.1 to 0.2% fatality rate, very similar to the flu and that has been well established now all over the world. But that still leaves one enduring mystery, why is there such a high death rate in nursing homes if the overall rate is so low? So for example Dr Marcus de Brun, recently of the Irish Medical Council, who has been very active on this estimates the death rate in the nursing home he dealt with in North County Dublin at about 12%, which is about 100 times the known fatality rate for this disease.[1] Obviously nursing home residents are likely to be older and sicker than the rest of the population, but to that degree, 100 times more likely to die? There must be some better reason for what is going on in the nursing homes in Ireland, and also in many other countries where they have been the particular bad spots for this disease, to explain which I will throw out the following possible theories.

Are lockdown measures causing deaths rather than preventing them?

If you consider it for a minute, the nursing homes were the most locked down element in the whole locked down country over the last few months in Ireland. They followed a policy of massively restricting visitors and stopped residents leaving the grounds from late February, certainly by the 6th of March, until it was somewhat eased on the 15th June. And it has been a particularly restrictive regime there for the residents, they were genuinely under house – if not room – arrest for all that time with no possibility of visitors whatsoever. Hence if the whole 'lockdown' was to work anywhere in halting this virus it would have worked in the nursing homes, and of course the complete opposite happened, it was much worse there than elsewhere.

Therefore it does not seem unreasonable to postulate that the whole lockdown policies are themselves spreading or deepening the fatality rate of this virus? There is a lot of literature out there that the widespread wearing of masks is harming peoples lungs and immune systems, which was probably more widely practiced in those homes, and stopping people going out into the fresh air to exercise could also be a factor in spreading rather than halting this disease. Also the impact on a person's morale of placing people under house arrest like this cannot be underestimated either, consider for example these reasons that a UK charity thinks might behind the recent increase in dementia deaths during the crisis:

> "The data, from the Office for National Statistics, reveals that, beyond deaths directly linked to Covid-19, there were 83% more deaths from dementia than usual in April, with charities warning that a reduction in essential medical care and family visits were taking a devastating toll.
>
> ...
>
> The charity thinks the increased numbers of deaths from dementia are resulting partly from increased cognitive impairment caused by isolation, the reduction in essential care as family carers cannot visit, and the onset of depression as people with dementia do not understand why loved ones are no longer visiting, causing them to lose skills and independence, such as the ability to speak or even stopping eating and drinking.
>
> Another factor may be interruptions to usual health services, with more than three-quarters of care homes reporting that GPs have been reluctant to visit residents." [2]

General care in the homes during the pandemic

That last point raises the issue of the overall quality of care, medical and otherwise, that the nursing home residents got during the pandemic. Unfortunately shocking stories have come out about this, and this general neglect might be itself a factor in the

deaths. Recently a carer in one of the homes in Ireland has come forward with a shocking picture of neglect, with residents confined to their rooms for days on end and even drenched in their own faeces and urine, she agrees that:
> "A lot of them could have been saved, yeah without a doubt." [3]

Medical Misadventure, including the flu vaccine

One simple point is that residents of nursing homes, and staff indeed, are much more likely to have received the influenza vaccine than the general population, and this could have made them more vulnerable to the virus according to some scientific papers on the subject. One expert on viruses, Dr. Judy Mikovitz, is quite clear on the subject:
> "If you have gotten a flu vaccine, that is driving the pandemic. You are likely to have gotten it from there...you get a flu vaccine today you amplify the problem." [4]

On the same subject of medical misadventure is the strange story of the recognised and quite successful treatment for Covid-19, which is hydroxychloroquine and zinc (and sometimes other drugs including antibiotics) administered early. It has transpired that there were a number of very large medical studies being conducted all over the world during the pandemic, into the success of hydroxychloroquine as a treatment. Under the auspices of the WHO and others, it involved giving Covid-19 patients hydroxychloroquine and studying the results.

What's strange about it is that they administered very large and, in the opinion of many experts, clearly fatal doses of the drug, and given late in the pathology of the disease, when the advocates of the drug had recommended much smaller doses given early on. It remains a mystery why these strangely high doses were given, was this done to artificially discredit this treatment? Or even to increase the death rate from Covid-19? [5]

Also it has been noted that the great hype and enthusiasm for mass producing hospital ventilators, which characterised the early months of this crisis, quite possibly put some patients on these machines who didn't need them. In fact some medical commentators are speculating now that many patients died because they were put on those machines.[6]

Euthanasia

This is a very dark subject, but could euthanasia, during all the hype about the disease, represent an explanation? In England it has been discovered that midazolam, a powerful drug frequently associated with 'end of life care', was prescribed something like 100% more often in the month of April than normal. Professor Patrick Pullicino, remarking on this and related advice given to health care professionals dealing with the crisis, states that:

> "...this flow chart encouraged use of end-of-life sedation with midazolam – effectively resulting in euthanasia pathways." [7]

This quote from a nurse in an Irish nursing home during the pandemic confirms the widespread use of the drug here in the context of those Covid-19 patients denied hospital care:

> "...who might possibly be saved by hospital transfer, and whose last comfort would be the inevitable cocktail of morphine and midazolam, slipped quietly under the skin at intervals until death arrives." [8]

Manipulation of the statistics

Finally we are of course assuming that the figures are correct, that a large number of nursing home residents died of Covid-19 during the pandemic. But actually there is widespread acknowledgement now that the figures have been manipulated, deliberately exaggerated during the pandemic, including in those figures nursing home residents and others who died of other causes. Even the then Taoiseach, Leo Varadkar, admits that the state 'skewed the numbers' at that time.[9]

Furthermore we are also assuming in these figures that the people who did test positive for the virus really had it, could spread it, or really suffered from it as such. There are actually serious question marks around all these issues with respect to the usual test for this virus, the RT-PCR test:

a) This test has always been vulnerable to showing false positives, in other words it could detect shards of DNA similar but not identical to the virus, especially as you increase the 'Cycle Threshold' for the test.[10]

b) One of the, many, primers – meaning a genetic sequence from the virus that you are checking against the sample being tested – used in the test for SARS-CoV-2 seems to be similar to what is already on chromosome 8 of the human genome.[11]

c) Because it is so sensitive it could detect the previous presence of the virus in a human who either long since threw off the disease or just never really suffered from it and is not an infectious carrier. This is especially true again if you are going to drill down and seek to detect the DNA through a large Cycle Threshold, which for some reason they are doing for this virus.[12]

After explaining the issues with this test, one medical expert recently went so far as to state:

> "So I would say, you know, that there is a 100%
> error rate with this test." [13]

Therefore the high death rate in the nursing homes is easily explained without impinging on our introductory thesis, that the state's response to the virus is grossly out of all reasonable or rational proportion.

Footnotes

1.   https://gript.ie/state-sanctioned-euthanasia-to-leave-covid-19-patients-in-infected-nursing-homes-says-doctor/ .

That Nursing Care Homes are the epicentre of this disease has been noted elsewhere:

> "In many countries, deaths in care homes account for 30 to 60% of all additional deaths. In Canada and some US states, care homes account for up to 80% of all "Covid19-related" deaths."
> (https://swprs.org/studies-on-covid-19-lethality/ .)

Ireland, with c.60% of all Covid-19 deaths being in nursing homes is the second highest proportion in the world after Canada. (Ibid.)

2.   https://www.theguardian.com/world/2020/jun/05/covid-19-causing-10000-dementia-deaths-beyond-infections-research-says .

Sunlight

As well as talking about the bad health consequences of the exaggerated fear of the virus, Dr Marcus de Brun, a GP in Rush Co. Dublin, author of *Being and Belonging* and holder of a degree in microbiology from TCD discusses further why some of the measures brought in to tackle the virus are likely to worsen its effects:

> "There is of course no controversy surrounding the assertion that UV exposure destroys viral particles.
>
> ...
>
> Locking a population indoors, where UV light is filtered out by glass, may not be as beneficial as is currently presumed. With an airborne or aerosol spread, transmission between homes may well be possible."
> (https://sway.office.com/PwTN7GCvJWDgn9yd?ref=Link&loc=play .)

Further on this important, and commonsensical, sunlight question:

> "In line with this notion, the authors took to note that the lockdowns within each country may adversely contributed to the success of the viral spread, notably with people who live in a multi-person household.
>
> "If we accept a possible virucidal role of sunlight during coronavirus pandemics, then forcing people to remain indoors may have increased (or assured) contagion of COVID-19 among same house-hold dwellers and among patients and personnel inside the same hospital or geriatric facilities," they said.
>
> Adding that "in contrast, healthy people outdoors receiving sunlight could have been exposed to lower viral dose with more chances for mounting an efficient immune response. This argument supports considering the results of

two opposed containment approaches to deal with the COVID-19 crisis.'"'
(	https://www.jpost.com/health-science/midday-sunlight-could-deactivate-up-to-90-percent-of-coronavirus-strain-study-632925 .)

masks
See:	https://www.youtube.com/watch?v=c4Hx5lntFwM	and https://jamesfetzer.org/2020/08/studies-of-surgical-masks-efficacy-masks-are-useless-in-preventing-the-spread-of-disease/ .
Also Dr Jenny Harris, the deputy Chief Medical Officer of England, says:
"'In fact, you can actually trap the virus in the mask and start breathing it in" and by wearing them "people can adversely put themselves at more risk than less."'
(	https://www.independent.co.uk/news/health/coronavirus-news-face-masks-increase-risk-infection-doctor-jenny-harries-a9396811.html .)

herd immunity
Noted here by Professor Michael Levitt, Professor of Structural Biology at the Stanford School of Medicine, and winner of the 2013 Nobel Prize for Chemistry:
"I think the policy of herd immunity is the right policy. I think Britain was on exactly the right track before they were fed wrong numbers. And they made a huge mistake. I see the standout winners as Germany and Sweden. They didn't practise too much lockdown and they got enough people sick to get some herd immunity. I see the standout losers as countries like Austria, Australia and Israel that had very strict lockdown but didn't have many cases. They have damaged their economies, caused massive social damage, damaged the educational year of their children, but not obtained any herd immunity.
"There is no doubt in my mind, that when we come to look back on this, the damage done by lockdown will exceed any saving of lives by a huge factor."
(	https://unherd.com/thepost/nobel-prize-winning-scientist-the-covid-19-epidemic-was-never-exponential/ .)
Dr Marcus de Brun who resigned form the Irish Medical Council over this, notes:
"Viral mutation within a population is an inevitability, and it is contingent upon time and the availability of hosts. Unfortunately, an unavoidable consequence of 'lock-down' and social distancing is that Herd-Immunity is effectively delayed, and in this sense an increasing amount of time is afforded to the virus permitting and possibly encouraging its

> mutation. In our efforts to delay the spread of the virus, the
> virus itself is afforded more time. This may well be good for
> us, but it is also 'good' for the virus."
> (https://sway.office.com/PwTN7GCvJWDgn9yd?
> ref=Link&loc=play .)

Could this be why:

> "Countries without curfews and contact bans, such as Japan,
> South Korea, Belarus or Sweden, have not experienced a
> more negative course of events than other countries. Sweden
> was even praised by the WHO and now benefits from higher
> immunity compared to lockdown countries."
> (https://swprs.org/a-swiss-doctor-on-covid-19/ .)

Also J P Morgan launched a study on the effects of the easing of the lockdowns and they found:

> "that many countries saw their infection rates fall rather than
> rise again when they ended their lockdowns – suggesting that
> the virus may have its own 'dynamics' which are 'unrelated'
> to the emergency measures."
>
> ...
>
> [Dr Marko] Kolanovic and his team [at the bank] also
> show that transmissibility of the virus has actually
> DECREASED after lockdowns have been lifted in U.S.
> states, through the measurement known as "RO". As the
> Daily Mail explains, "many states saw a lower rate of
> transmission (R) after full-scale lockdowns were ended."
> (https://childrenshealthdefense.org/news/lockdown-lunacy-
> the-thinking-persons-guide/ .)

3. https://www.youtube.com/watch?v=rRzABh6F9AM 13:23.
From one nursing home in Meath a resident was transferred to hospital because the home was 'unable to manage', his neglect even included facial maggots: https://www.rte.ie/news/2020/0706/1151737-ultan-meehan-kilbrew-home/ .

Also the vast majority of Covid-19 infected nursing home patients were not transferred to – largely empty – acute hospitals, which presumably reflects how little care was taken to save their lives. Hence while "one in six nursing home residents who contracted Covid-19 died" nonetheless "of those infected in nursing homes...just 5% were hospitalised." (*The Irish Times* 2/5/2020, Weekend Review p.1.)

This point is confirmed by George Lee, the RTE correspondent on the crisis:

> "Out of the 1,944 confirmed COVID19 cases found in
> nursing homes, only 190 have been treated in hospital. 450
> have died."
> (https://twitter.com/GeorgeLeeRTE/status/12532184463195
> 38176 .)

Dr Marcus de Brun, who worked in an Irish nursing home during this period described how they were denied basic medical tests, so they couldn't diagnose the different diseases, and treatments:

> "So for a full three weeks in the height of the crisis the people who needed testing were denied testing, and people are scratching their heads now wondering why we have had over a thousand deaths in nursing homes and why it has been the vast majority of people in Ireland who have died [of this disease] in nursing homes, when those people themselves were denied tests, denied oxygen, denied the basic fundamentals of medicine."
> (Dave Cullen interview 5/6/2020:
> https://www.youtube.com/watch?v=2AR7__YmVBE 17:32.)

4. *The Raw Deal with Jim Fitzer,* 29th April 2020, https://ln2.sync.com/dl/a18607190/xmixqqwi-w7rzr2td-gt9miv5c-bmv89re9/view/default/4081216820010 32:34.
Professor Dolores Cahill, who actually ran one of these advanced virus laboratories like in Wuhan, agrees with Dr. Judy Mikovitz, particularly with reference to the use of monkey cells in the creation of the flu vaccine:

> "I agree entirely with Judy."
> (https://www.youtube.com/watch?v=y-NdcOBJyW8 0:51.)

A study by Gregg Wolff of records of about 5,000 US military personnel, and published in the January 2020 edition of *Vaccine* magazine noted:

> "Examining noninfluenza viruses specifically, the odds of both coronavirus and human metapneumovirus in vaccinated individuals were significantly higher when compared to unvaccinated individuals (OR = 1.36 and 1.51, respectively) (Table 5). Conversely, all other non-influenza respiratory viruses had decreased odds in the vaccinated population
>
> ...
>
> Additionally, the laboratory data in our study showed increased odds of coronavirus and human metapneumovirus in individuals receiving influenza vaccination."
> (https://www.ncbi.nlm.nih.gov/pmc/articles/PMC7126676/pdf/main.pdf .)

The medical/media establishment are busy 'fact checking' this study because of its obvious implications for the pandemic but their criticisms are so weak they more reinforce the importance of the study, rather than the opposite, I would say: https://eu.usatoday.com/story/news/factcheck/2020/04/01/fact-check-flu-shot-coronavirus-not-connected-medical-experts-say/2933900001/   and https://healthfeedback.org/claimreview/claim-that-flu-vaccine-increases-coronavirus-infection-is-unsupported-misinterprets-scientific-studies/ .

See also Benjamin Cowling et alios, *Increased Risk of Noninfluenza Respiratory Virus Infections Associated with Receipt of Inactivated Influenza Vaccine,* Clinical Infectious Diseases, 15 March 2012.

5. See: http://www.francesoir.fr/politique-monde/uk-therapeutic-approach-covid-19-flawed-yet-it-can-still-be-rectified?fbclid=IwAR0zHjLcfipOll-cz8xfrY-xWNmzfWRgbVI_R5MrXcBLcvWDn9vGQMWLifl .

As you can read in that French newspaper, an Irishman, Robert Nugent, has done a lot of the running tracking down the details of this treatment and you see more about it on his youtube channel: https://www.youtube.com/channel/UCiraYLOOluPut1EZopwM0RA/videos , twitter account: https://twitter.com/RobertANugent1 , and facebook page: https://www.facebook.com/robertnugent . To give some detail on this:

> "The deputy Chief Investigator of the Recovery Trials, Professor Martin Landray gave an interview to FranceSoir. What he revealed was quite remarkable.
>
> Firstly, the mortality rate of the hydroxychloroquine patients was a staggering 25.7%.
>
> The recommended hydroxychloroquine dose for an adult in the UK is no more than 200 – 400mg per day. In France 1800mg per day is considered to be lethal poisoning.
>
> Across 175 UK hospitals, 1542 patient participants in the Recovery Trials were given 2400mg (six times the recommended maximum dose) in the first twenty-four hours. This was followed up by ten days at twice the recommended maximum dose at 800mg.
>
> It isn't really clear what the objective was. This wasn't so much a trial of effectiveness, it looked more like an experiment in toxic poisoning. It would seem to account for the atrocious mortality rate."
>
> (http://www.thetruthseeker.co.uk/?p=209051 .)

Some further information:

> "Even worse, a series of hydroxychloroquine studies that appeared to be designed for failure by issuing the drug by itself, issuing it way too late in the infection's progression in a patient, or issuing it at inappropriate high dosages, were quickly conducted. Many of the "studies" where cancelled as they began to unsurprisingly fail. These failures furthered the narrative of Hydroxychloroquine's ineffectiveness for COVID-19 and the media wasted no time or headline space drumming home this message."
>
> (https://www.thegatewaypundit.com/2020/07/despite-media-lies-study-shows-hydroxychloroquine-can-provide-50-70-chance-recovery-china-coronavirus/ .)

6. Dr Andrew Kaufman MD:

> "I think what's happening is that anybody that is being labelled as a Covid, there are really two separate issues:
>
> One is that there is some strong evidence that they are neglecting those patients. Right they are probably afraid of

them [medical professionals afraid of getting the disease themselves]. They are not doing codes, they are doing things like a slow code [meaning they deliberately respond to calls to treat those patients slowly, in order that they will die because they consider deaths in those cases to be inevitable.]...but they are doing this for Covid patients even if they are not you know so direly ill, because maybe they are afraid of getting infected.

But they have also changed all the protocols for breathing support...They have skipped all of the preliminary steps to support breathing and oxygenation and go right to the ventilator. And we know that this is motivated mainly by the financial incentives of earning three times as much money, based on medicare reimbursement, for using a ventilator. But also its because the ventilator is a closed system and they are worried about, you know, the possible respiratory contagion, you know through the airborne contagion, so they skip all these steps but as a result of that they are actually causing lots of morbidity and mortality. The ventilators are not a friendly procedure to use and besides that I have heard that most of these patients are awake and alert and even comfortable, they are not even in respiratory distress. So you basically have to provide general anaesthesia in order to even put them on the ventilator because they will be fighting against their chest being automatically inflated. So you have, putting them on general anaesthesia increases the risk for mortality, morbidity, things like blood clots, pulmonary embolism, which we have seen in a lot of autopsy reports. Right and then you get ventilator lung injury so I wonder if there is actually more people dying of those hospital procedures now."
(https://www.youtube.com/watch?v=OnFqkFS4K-A 48:43.)

Also this nurse has raised the issue, Erin Marie Olszewski in New York, who also hints at a type off euthanasia. She was asked by the interviewer about a 37 old who died and was treated for Covid-19 even though his tests stated he didn't have it:

"What killed him? Was being, did the vent kill him?"
"Yeah, oh yes, they are so sedated he had probably 8 or 9 drugs, its all sedation, its all sedation and paralytics. So you are asleep, it is essentially like you're under, you know like in surgery. You know when they put you under like that, emm, for a good month, straight. There is no way you can recover from something like that. You are brain dead if you do."
(https://www.youtube.com/watch?
time_continue=4&v=InwxVlKbSQ0&feature=emb_title

21:09.)
This issue is causing some disquiet in the medical literature:

> "But some health professionals have wondered whether the breathing machines might actually make matters worse in certain patients, perhaps by igniting or worsening a harmful immune system reaction.
>
> That's speculation. But experts do say ventilators can be damaging to a patient over time, as high-pressure oxygen is forced into the tiny air sacs in a patient's lungs.
>
> "We know that mechanical ventilation is not benign," said Dr. Eddy Fan, an expert on respiratory treatment at Toronto General Hospital. "One of the most important findings in the last few decades is that medical ventilation can worsen lung injury..."
>
> (https://www.modernhealthcare.com/safety-quality/some-doctors-moving-away-ventilators-virus-patients .)

7. Stephen Adams and Holly Bancroft, *Did care homes use powerful sedative to speed Covid deaths?*, Mail on Sunday 13/07/2020, p.33, https://twitter.com/EileenC27535831/status/1282434124884717568 .

8. https://www.rte.ie/culture/2020/0429/1135577-nursing-home-chaos-diary-of-a-pandemic-doctor/ .

Noeleen, a friend of Gemma O'Doherty's, described how the HSE were very anxious to get non resuscitation orders signed recently, and also described how her uncle, who died in a nursing home during the pandemic, was mysteriously prescribed large does of morphine: https://www.youtube.com/watch?v=-8_p2jQh2N0 .

These Do Not Resusitate (DNR) forms have, in the opinion of some knowledgeable experts including Dr Vernon Coleman (https://www.youtube.com/watch?v=AtddJr90Tg0), morphed into permission for euthanasia, as one Irish commentator noted during the pandemic:

> "Spare a thought for the elderly who were handed DNR forms to sign in Public Nursing homes, denied suitable care and left to die from dyhydration. maybe think of your parents in that position...when you look to hand extra power to the HSE."
>
> (https://twitter.com/Caro50886110/status/995612834049482752 .)

Another example from a whistle blower carer in a nursing home in England:

> "They have put all our residents on Do Not Resuscitate orders, and all of these residents with variable or lack of capacity are on anticipatory care pathways, which means that they are not allowed to go to hospital for any treatment for anything and they aren't to receive any antibiotics for

anything whatsoever, whatever illness they have got.

Since this 'pandemic' started we haven't had a single GP visit the patients at our home. Whenever anyone gets ill, and this is ill[ness] not related to Covid because we haven't got it in my care home, they automatically put them on end of life and nil by mouth and they discontinue all their medication because they say they are at risk of aspiration. Which is ridiculous because if they eat, drink or have medication there is a small chance that they could aspirate but if they are nil by mouth then they will die from dehydration and starvation.

...

Along with this the GPs are remotely prescribing end of life medication, which is morphine and midazolam injections and these are being misused.

All our clients have had their usual medication taken away, which is regular pain relief such as paracetemol and codeine and all their anxiety anti-depression and anti-psychotic medication, which a lot of our clients are on. The district nurses then come in to the home to give end of life drugs because with the withdrawal of the usual medication the resident is showing signs of pain and anxiety, which of course they would."
(https://www.bitchute.com/video/KfqJvRhKqH8e/ 4:40 and 6:36.)

9. Leo Varadkar:

"In Ireland we counted all deaths, in all settings, suspected cases even when no lab test was done, and included people with underlying terminal illnesses who died with Covid but not of it. This was right approach but skewed the numbers."
(https://twitter.com/LeoVaradkar/status/1278995351169613824 .)

This is in the context of a recent report from the Health Information and Quality Authority:

"Excess deaths in Ireland from March to June were "substantially" less than the officially reported Covid-19 figures, analysis from the Health Information and Quality Authority has found.

HIQA says this could be due to the inclusion within official figures of people who were infected with coronavirus but whose cause of death may have been predominantly due to other factors.

Excess deaths refers to the number of deaths over and above what would normally be expected for that time of year.

...

The implication then is that the official daily figure which

was 1,709 may overstate the actual excess deaths due to Covid-19 by 59.4%."
(https://www.rte.ie/news/health/2020/0703/1151127-virus-report/ .)

Its also an issue internationally, here for example is Dr Andrew Kaufman replying to a question asking why the CDC issued a document asking doctors to 'assume' deaths from Covid-19 on their death certificates:

"This is a major departure from the normal policy of how you fill out a death certificate...They didn't just use the word assume, they used the word suspicion. So like if you 'suspect' covid then you are supposed to put it as the cause of death.

So this is so obvious as just a method to inflate the numbers, but they took it even further and they have, and I don't know if the CDC did this but this might be a state by state policy but I saw a letter in New Jersey to this affect and I have heard about the same process in other states, and even in other countries, where:

Normally during a health crisis or health emergency situation right, which is what has been declared and that's the official justification for taking away our first amendment rights, they are supposed to send all of the cases of the public health, you know all the cases of people who died from whatever the crisis is, to the coroner for autopsy, because they need to get to the bottom of what is going on. Now in this situation they specifically instructed *not* to send any bodies for autopsies. So that is basically to hide the fact that they would find other causes of death."
(https://www.youtube.com/watch?v=OnFqkFS4K-A 1:39:13.)

10. As even Public Health England have noted with respect to this virus:
"It is important to note that detecting viral material by PCR does not indicate that the virus is fully intact and infectious, i.e. able to cause infection in other people."
(https://www.reuters.com/article/uk-factcheck-pcr/fact-check-inventor-of-method-used-to-test-for-covid-19-didnt-say-it-cant-be-used-in-virus-detection-idUSKBN24420X .)

11. https://www.youtube.com/watch?v=TgVdjAgg2J0 14:24.

12. This is explained in detail at the Oxford Centre for Evidence-Based Medicine site here: https://www.cebm.net/covid-19/infectious-positive-pcr-test-result-covid-19/ . That they are using remarkably high Cycle Threshold's in detecting this virus is confirmed by the *New York Times*: "You're Positive. But Are You Contagious? Tests May Be Too Sensitive, Experts Say," by

Apoorva Mandavilli, 30/08/2020, Section A page 6, from which:

> "The standard tests are diagnosing huge numbers of people who may be carrying relatively insignificant amounts of the virus.
>
> ...
>
> In three sets of testing data that include cycle thresholds, compiled by officials in Massachusetts, New York and Nevada, up to 90 percent of people testing positive carried barely any virus, a review by The Times found.
>
> ...
>
> On Thursday, the United States recorded 45,604 new coronavirus cases, according to a database maintained by The Times. If the rates of contagiousness in Massachusetts and New York were to apply nationwide, then perhaps only 4,500 of those people may actually need to isolate and submit to contact tracing.
>
> ...
>
> One solution would be to adjust the cycle threshold used now to decide that a patient is infected. Most tests set the limit at 40, a few at 37. This means that you are positive for the coronavirus if the test process required up to 40 cycles, or 37, to detect the virus.
>
> Tests with thresholds so high may detect not just live virus but also genetic fragments, leftovers from infection that pose no particular risk — akin to finding a hair in a room long after a person has left, Dr. Mina said.
>
> Any test with a cycle threshold above 35 is too sensitive, agreed Juliet Morrison, a virologist at the University of California, Riverside. "I'm shocked that people would think that 40 could represent a positive," she said."
> (https://www.nytimes.com/2020/08/29/health/coronavirus-testing.html .)

13. Dr Andrew Kaufman interviewed here: https://www.youtube.com/watch?v=TgVdjAgg2J0 20:26.

CHAPTER 2
Some worldwide acknowledgement that the lockdown was a deadly and unnecessary over reaction

Alright so clearly we should never have had any lockdown, and the measures in place now should be rescinded, a fact that, putting the mad world of the mass media to one side, I think most patriotically minded citizens all over the world can see. And indeed this is penetrating a little bit into the higher reaches of officialdom.

John Oxford, the Professor of Virology at Queen Mary, University of London:

> "Personally, I would say the best advice is to spend less time watching TV news which is sensational and not very good. Personally, I view this Covid outbreak as akin to a bad winter influenza epidemic. In this case we have had 8000 deaths this last year in the 'at risk' groups viz over 65% people with heart disease etc. I do not feel this current Covid will exceed this number. We are suffering from a media epidemic!" [1]

On May 26th Dr Alexander Myasnikov, 'the head of Russia's Covid-19 monitoring centre', in a recorded aside at the end of an interview stated:

> "It's all bullshit…It's all exaggerated. It's an acute respiratory disease with minimal mortality…Why has the whole world been destroyed? That I don't know." [2]

Also the German Department of the Interior commissioned a scientific panel of medical experts from several German universities to produce what became a 93 page report called an *Analysis of the Crisis Management* on the whole German response to the pandemic. Some of its conclusions include:

> "– The dangerousness of Covid-19 was overestimated: probably at no point did the danger posed by the new virus go beyond the normal level.

– The danger is obviously no greater than that of many other viruses. There is no evidence that this was more than a false alarm.

– During the Corona crisis the State has proved itself as one of the biggest producers of Fake News." [3]

Yes the government report really did say that, although of course it was soon suppressed etc. So ok what happened was clearly very wrong, this whole disproportionate over reaction to the virus, but is that all it is? I wonder how many of the aforementioned 'patriotically minded citizens' would go a step further. Was this just an over reaction to the pandemic, driven by fear and exaggerated international media reports, or is there something more sinister happening?

I respectfully submit that what you are seeing here is a consolidation of power by, what used to be called, Communists. The worldwide experience of Communism gives us our best insight into the thinking of globalists, who are I think pushing their agenda using the pandemic as cover. To explain this lets just look at the principles and practices of Communism and compare that to what is happening now.

Footnotes
1.   https://novuscomms.com/2020/03/31/a-view-from-the-hvivo-open-orphan-orph-laboratory-professor-john-oxford/ .

2.   https://off-guardian.org/2020/05/31/its-all-bullsht-3-leaks-that-sink-the-covid-narrative/ .

3.   Ibid, and you can read more details on it here: https://www.thetruthseeker.co.uk/?p=208180 .

CHAPTER 3
The Communist policies pursued during the pandemic

This analysis is of the "by their fruits you shall know them" type. In other words it does not speculate on precisely 'who' is pushing this, or indeed 'how', but it will hopefully demonstrate the reality that these policies are being enthusiastically pursued now. That itself, I believe, shows the instigators must be Communists, because they are pursuing Communist policies.

Dependency on the State

Obviously under Communism money and jobs flow through the state almost exclusively, the state employs you or at least any money you receive comes from the state. In theory this was designed to make everything equal and fair, in practice it was to create a dependency by the ordinary people onto the state, which the corrupt Communists controlled. Hence you could not sustain yourself or your family if you fell out with your Communist masters.

It is increasingly the case in modern Ireland that nobody earns an economic wage unless they work for the state, or receive some state subvention directly or indirectly, or they work for some large multinational, who in turn work closely with the state. There is no real middle ground left, the SME sector is crushed by the sheer uneconomic reality of their jobs, squeezed as they are by overwhelming state regulations and taxes.

And this effect has gone into overdrive during the pandemic, the state regulations on social distancing and quarantines etc on the one hand, plus the inability to compete on wages with those receiving the special Covid-19 direct payments or wage subsidies on the other, have simply decimated the SME sector in Ireland.[1] And this, I respectfully submit, is actually no accident, it creates that dependency for your livelihood on corrupt entities which was always a great feature of Communism.

State Surveillance by Intelligence Agencies

Of course massively powerful intelligence agencies, with their all embracing surveillance capabilities are another great characteristic of Communist countries. The KGB in the Soviet Union and the Stasi in East Germany have become a byword for that kind of overarching state security apparatus and control.

This again is another phenomenon which has been growing for quite a while in Ireland but its rocketed in its reach during the pandemic. Social outlets, including pubs and restaurants, are now encouraged to take the details of anybody using their premises, people returning from flights also have to log their movements on special new forms which you can be sure will be integrated into the security apparatus, while there were even reports of local authorities in Ireland using drones to spy on people during the pandemic. Meanwhile we already have a special Covid-19 tracing app installed on virtually all mobile phones (the API for the app was downloaded with the latest updates to both iphone and android phones, this is installed automatically and is then used by the Irish Covid app) which tracks everybody everywhere in real time using bluetooth etc.[2] The authorities are trying to drag everybody into this state surveillance as can be seen from an Irish teacher, Diomsigh Ní Deirdra, talking about the new training they have received before the schools reopen:

> "...we were told to police one another and the parents, to report any parents you felt were anti the mainstream stories." [3]

The era we live in, with mobile phones, credit cards (much more widely used during the pandemic, in some cases with shops refusing cash) cctv cameras, important meetings held via Zoom, etc, all of which are clearly integrated into the collection apparatus of the big Western intelligence agencies, has created surveillance capabilities such that the Stasi could have only dreamed of, and again sent into over drive by the measures the state took during the pandemic.

As a witness that these huge Western intelligence agencies really are like the Stasi I call William Binney, after 30 years in the

National Security Agency (NSA) and military intelligence he was appointed in 1997 the Technical Director of the NSA, with a full global remit overseeing some 6,000 analysts, and he states:

> "I had worked the Soviet Union problem for almost thirty years and it was very clear to me that in October 2001 the NSA and government, the US government, started adopting the procedures and techniques and processes that the Soviet Union and the Stasi and all of the countries behind the Iron Curtain were using, and so we were actually adopting their procedures. It was very clear to me that was what was going on." [4]

He is not alone seeing the comparison, Brian Gerrish, who worked as a Royal Naval intelligence officer during the Cold War describes the recent Covid-19 powers of the UK government:

> "I have got to say, this is Soviet, its the Conservative Party introducing what all my professional training says is Soviet policy, quite amazing." [5]

Deliberately Fragmenting Communities and Populations

Another element that the Communist authorities took aim at was to target close knit communities and nations with a view to breaking them up. It was obviously easier for the authorities to control societies that lacked community cohesion and identity, so for example they frequently compelled native populations to move from their homelands, such as the Chechens and countless other races in the Soviet Union, or encouraged the movement of native Russians into areas with populations considered potentially problematical. An example of the latter would be the encouragement of native Russian migration to the Baltic States, which had been independent in the early 20th century.

But they went further than this, you can trace I believe an overall pattern where they sought to atomise community structures overall in society. You see for them the science of political control is how to control crowds and networks of people, and basically stop any groups forming, that way you can always keep a lid on society, its much easier for the state to clamp down on an individual on his/her own rather than having to deal with close knit groups or communities.[6]

Obviously you can see where this is going, the 'social distancing' idea, a lynchpin of the state's response to the pandemic, is entirely out of this Communist playbook. Consider this short tale of modern day traveling and ask yourself what effect it will have on sustaining a tight knit community atmosphere:

> "We passengers are busier tracking and tracing each other's footwork, pivoting to see ahead and behind while remaining all ears for a fellow traveller's sneeze or a suggestive throat clear. It has certainly changed the usual friendly holiday banter.
>
> "Move back, mate, thanks."
>
> "Watch the kids there, please Mum."
>
> "Six feet! Six feet!"
>
> The latter is screamed by a woman at a teenage boy, who is standing, just as she is, on suitably spaced labels on the floor. He looks around helplessly for support, but none of us meets his eye or offers a word. He shrugs. She flaps. We all silently look downward, together.
>
> No signage can direct us to the appropriate social niceties and human decencies that have been killed off by our communal fear of catching Covid. No official messaging speaks to our isolation from each other these days, ..." [7]

Here is a similar perspective from John D. Walsh, a long term political activist from Waterford:

> "I went to Supervalu at the Tramore roundabout last week. Nearly everybody had a mask there unlike the previous two shops I was in. It was like being part of an episode of the Twilight Zone (I am thinking of two episodes: The Masks; and Pig Masks) where you are normal and everybody

around you is behaving abnormally. I reached out for my TV remote control but this was REAL! It was so oppressive as eyes glared towards you as if from George Orwell's 1984 novel! It was so terrifying I could not get out fast enough!

...

Social distancing is profoundly anti-Christian and is the foundation of hostility. If you muzzle a dog, he can get very cross. We are all seen as potential infectors and therefore an enemy. Approaching a stranger, you are likely to be snapped at and treated with contempt. Normal friendly relations are gone out the window. Masks deprive us of our humanity and render us futile in communicating with others tenderly." [8]

You can see how much this dovetails beautifully with long established Communist aims and practices. Great thinkers have always known this, for example Hannah Arendt in her famous 1958 study of how totalitarian governments can arise and succeed:

"It has frequently been observed that terror can rule absolutely only over men who are isolated against each other and that, therefore, one of the primary concerns of all tyrannical government is to bring this isolation about. Isolation may be the beginning of terror; it certainly is its most fertile ground; it always is its result. This isolation is, as it were, pretotalitarian; its hallmark is impotence insofar as power always comes from men acting together, "acting in concert" (Burke); isolated men are powerless by definition." [9]

Oppression of the Church

Obviously Communism made nearly all religions, but particularly the Christian religion and especially Catholicism, its public enemy number one. Again this was all justified on the grounds of the Church supposedly oppressing the masses in the past etc, but actually the reason they really needed to destroy the Church was because it held out a separate set of values to the state sponsored ones.

You see brainwashing, of one type or another, is an essential component of the Communist state and to do that, to get the populations to surrender body and soul to the state, you need to strip out of people their existing value system in order to implant the Communist one. If people are going to continue to think that lying or murder etc are very wrong, i.e. Christian values, then you cannot manipulate them as much as when they have no other moral yardstick to follow than just the state laws and regulations.

I respectfully submit that you can see this oppressive atmosphere towards the Catholic Church very visibly in modern Ireland. Every other year some massively hyped 'scandal' arises (while there were some real scandals originally, like Fr Brendan Smyth, the inverted commas are now justified) which leads more Irish people to run away from the Church and embrace atheism, the best attitude to take for the 'brainwashing' to implant itself.

Its also obvious that this effect is again energised enormously during this pandemic. For some reason, I would suggest for the above reason, Church activities seem to be most targeted by the State for suppression during the pandemic.[10] For instance, as this is written, in early August 2020, we seem to be in the most open period, the least locked down, of this pandemic (because there is a lot of talk of the state reintroducing their lockdown measures shortly). But even now, virtually all First Holy Communion, Confirmation and Cemetery Sunday celebrations/events have been cancelled or at least postponed all across the Catholic Church in Ireland. All pilgrimages, known to this writer at any rate, have ceased, including Lough Derg for the first time since 1828, the Knock Novena and the most important feast day at that shrine, Croagh Patrick, although a few ignored the closure and went anyway, and Portiuncula, an important Franciscan pilgrimage cancelled as well. There are enormous restrictions on weddings and funerals and Churches are littered with the familiar government yellow posters mandating 'social distancing' with lay members of many Churches turning away parishioners from masses as part of these restrictions. These posters and measures seem way more prominent in Churches than any other institution across Ireland.

This again is during the most open time in 2020 pandemic Ireland, the time with the least restrictions. During the lockdown itself virtually all Church activities of any type ceased completely. Those few Churches who tried to keep some sacraments available, such as the SSPX Churches in Athlone and Mounttown in Dublin, were closely monitored and routinely visited by the Gardaí. This writers rural parish priest even found himself in communication with the Gardaí when a few too many turned up to a funeral.

All this has given rise to the following plaintive plea from Catríona Collins:

> "Is there any church in Dublin not a dystopian nightmare. Was the only unmasked person in my Anti-social & distanced church today, trying to hide my tears and not sniffle, obvs. It's become a heartbreaking ordeal to go. The priest gave a homily on...racism." [11]

Again and again, you can see that the way society is changing in 2020 is very reminiscent of the old Communist world, and not accidentally.

Footnotes

1. In the US federal authorities give the newly unemployed $600 a week on top of whatever state benefits they get which means that two thirds of these workers get more now than when they were working:

> "If these benefits were extended through January 2021, five of every six recipients would receive more in benefits than they would from working those six months, according to the Congressional Budget Office."
> (https://www.marketwatch.com/story/the-extra-600-americans-get-in-weekly-unemployment-benefits-ends-next-month-heres-what-lawmakers-are-proposing-to-replace-it-2020-06-09 .)

In Ireland 40% of those getting the Covid-19 payment were earning less when they worked: https://www.todayfm.com/news/almost-40-people-covid-payment-earning-less-e300-week-1018529 , also see *Sunday Times* 24/5/2020, p.15.

Spain has introduced a basic income which will 'stay forever', Scotland is also proposing such a scheme:

> "A universal basic income scheme would see a government pay out monthly stipends to every citizen, regardless of their financial or employment status."

Even in the US these proposals are 'regardless of employment status', the state will simple hand people c.$2,000 a month if you are on less than $130,000 a year.
(https://www.businessinsider.com/spain-to-approve-basic-income-scheme-response-coroanvirus-outbreak-2020-5?r=US&IR=T   and https://www.businessnewsdaily.com/9649-universal-basic-income-business-impact.html .)

2.

> "The [Irish contact tracing] app will remain working in the background regardless of whether or not someone chooses to close it."
> (https://www.irishexaminer.com/breakingnews/ireland/qanda-what-you-need-to-know-about-the-new-covid-tracker-smartphone-app-1009867.html .)
> "Professor [Douglas] Leith [of Trinity College Dublin] says he is very concerned by these revelations.
>
> "Governments and public health authorities are strongly encouraging their entire populations to use these apps. In a sense they are pressurising their entire populations to take part in this corporate surveillance."
> (https://www.breakingnews.ie/ireland/covid-app-leaking-personal-data-to-google-say-trinity-researchers-1011945.html .)

3. https://twitter.com/fionamflanagan1/status/1293965540734701578/photo/1 .

4. https://www.youtube.com/watch?v=xF_VYNtDgN8 10:49, you can read more about Binney here:
https://www.pbs.org/wgbh/pages/frontline/government-elections-politics/united-states-of-secrets/the-frontline-interview-william-binney/ .
William Binney also describes how the current system is much worse than COINTELPRO, – which was an FBI program, while the NSA had MINARET and the CIA had CHAOS –:
> "Its the same three agencies today doing the same thing but on a much larger more comprehensive scale."
>
> ...
>
> Chris Hedges: This intelligence becomes actionable, in terms of carrying out dirty tricks.
>
> William Binney: Yeah, yeah, it gives you leverage, once you know about everybody, what they are doing, what they are thinking, what they are planning, I mean you have the opportunity to manipulate them any way you want. By causing certain things to occur, making certain suggestions in certain areas or you know just simply outright blackmail against them or anything that you can leverage against them or anything that they, against somebody they really care about. So you have an opportunity to do all of that."
>
> (https://www.youtube.com/watch?v=vHb1Zebr2is , 18:06 talking about Cointelpro etc, 18:28 discussion about 'actionable' intelligence, at 19:29 he talks about the kind of devices that could cause ill health in targeted people.)

This COINTELPRO type tactic – where the state uses the information it gathers by mass surveillance to destroy peoples lives even if they haven't broken the law – was even used against him:
> "Every time we tried to do something in business they sent the FBI after us, so they were trying to put us out of business permanently."
>
> (https://www.pbs.org/wgbh/pages/frontline/government-elections-politics/united-states-of-secrets/the-frontline-interview-william-binney/ 34:50.)

Also:
> "They basically made our lives a mess, they made us incapable of getting business so, so that kind of thing is the power that they have. They can harass you in many different ways and so they tried doing that with us."
>
> (https://www.youtube.com/watch?v=59H1vu9IlhM 30:36.)

Here again he refers to how the state uses the information:
> "[The enormous quantities involved in the bulk acquisition of data is not focused enough to be really helpful in combating terrorism etc]...but it gives them a great set of information to

control their population if they want to do it. Also to do things like industrial espionage, all the bidding would be in there in the encrypted data and they get through the encryption which I don't think would be too much difficulty, then they could see the bidding and break the outcome. So there is that plus they are gathering information on every leader in every government of the world. So that means they have information to be able to blackmail everybody. This data is not just used by the NSA, this is the FBI, the DEA (Drug Enforcement Administration), going directly into that data with no oversight or recording at all by anybody. They use it for policing issues and so on inside the United States and around the world and its not being monitored, there is no oversight of that at all and there is no admission in a court of law anywhere in the world that they are doing that. So in other words they perjure themselves in a court of law."
(https://www.youtube.com/watch?v=mzhj2xUXLmg 4:26.)

You can follow his career in the NSA in the film *A Good American*, at one time his group's budget was 1.4 billion dollars: https://www.youtube.com/watch?v=666wsDcoNrU .

This link describes how the US state had planned, a few months before the pandemic hit, to use new surveillance technologies copying the Chinese: https://thelastamericanvagabond.com/top-news/techno-tyranny-how-us-national-security-state-using-coronavirus-fulfill-orwellian-vision/ .

Technology already rolled out in latest updates to android and apple mobile phones: https://www.cnbc.com/2020/05/20/three-states-commit-to-apple-google-technology-for-virus-tracking-apps.html .

Contact tracing is slated to employ c.300,000 people in the USA, spying on people allegedly because of the virus: https://technocracy.news/the-miserable-pseudo-science-behind-face-masks-social-distancing-and-contact-tracing/ .

5. *UK Column News*, 5 August 2020, https://www.youtube.com/watch?v=D_7aAlMc_3I 9:17.

6. For example in a 2008 work which sought to establish if traditional Communist practices were implemented in modern Ireland, this policy was speculated on:

"Isolationisation
According to Julianne McKinney, who served as a US intelligence agent in Berlin during the Cold War, the Soviet Union had a policy of trying to "divide and isolate the populace" in order to maintain its control over the subject peoples of the Soviet Union. The thinking here was that strong community structures made it difficult for the KGB to isolate those dissidents that they wished to harass, so where possible they would prefer to break down those communities

everywhere.

Again if you look at Rossport you can see why a government might feel threatened by communities and groups much more than by individuals. What started there was that about two people initially dug their heels in and opposed the pipeline, then in court about five people were prepared to go to jail rather than be bullied by the system, then after they were jailed maybe about 1,000 people in the same community rose up and challenged the authorities. Its obvious that when you have a strong community that sticks together like this then the government has much more problems than in those parts of Ireland where people have been jailed in almost total community silence and anonymity. Its the existence of a tight knit community itself that causes problems for the state, it would be much better from their point of view if people didn't have wide circles of friends, family or neighbours that will defend each other. You need to isolate people to crush them. I believe that governments at a high level know this very well..."
(*Orwellian Ireland* (Corstown, 2008), p.228.)

7. Pat Murray, *The Sunday Times* 5/7/2020, Travel Supplement, p.11.

8. Facebook page of his son Pádraic Walsh: https://www.facebook.com/photo?fbid=2883712308406247&set=pcb.2883716251739186 .

9. Hannah Arendt, *The Origins of Totalitarianism* (New York, 1958, second edition), p.474,
https://www.nypl.org/sites/default/files/arendt_originsoftotalitarianism.pdf .

10. Recently in Wisconsin they attempted to enforce a complete ban on over 50 person Church services while imposing no restrictions at all on BLM marches:

"Following its May 22 order, the Madison/Dane County Health Department multiple times called and visited Diocesan officials and parishes to inform them that surveillance officials would be sent to churches and fines of up to $1000 would be imposed for every instance in which more than 50 people were gathered for Mass."
(https://www.lifesitenews.com/news/wisconsin-govt-changes-course-lifts-special-restrictions-on-catholics-after-bishops-outcry .)

While a member of the national federal government Covid-19 committee in Canada, Dr Robert Strang, also the Chief Medical Officer of Nova Scotia, is talking about further restricting Church activities for about two more years. Even Human Rights groups in Canada, such as the Calgary-based Justice Centre for Constitutional Freedoms (JCCF) through their lawyer Lisa Bildy, are noticing this:

> "Bildy pointed out that governments have placed more severe restrictions on churches than other sectors...."Faith groups apparently cannot be...trusted.""
> (https://www.lifesitenews.com/news/churches-may-not-return-to-full-capacity-for-1-2-years-nova-scotia-top-doc-says .)

In a rare example of courts enforcing religious liberty rights during this pandemic, a New York judge pointed out the anomaly of politicians claiming to close down religious services for public health reasons while simultaneously supporting mass Black Lives Matter protests, a situation that exists graphically in Ireland too:

> "The hypocrisy of the radically liberal Cuomo and de Blasio has finally been officially exposed. Judge Sharpe chastised the liberal politicians for persecuting religious gatherings on the pretext of public health while commending and even joining mass outdoor protests, many of which resulted in looting and violence. Sharpe blasted de Blasio's argument that his banning of even outdoor religious ceremonies was motivated by public safety concerns while lauding the mass protests. Such action, according to Sharpe, "clearly undermine the legitimacy" of de Blasio's claim."
> (https://catholicfamilynews.com/blog/2020/06/26/breaking-cfn-contributor-chris-ferrara-obtains-early-victory-against-new-yorks-persecution-of-the-church/ .)

11.   https://twitter.com/CatrionaColllns/status/1294982199561912320 16/8/2020.

CHAPTER 4
Objections to this portrayal of Ireland as a Communist/Orwellian state

But of course the average reader of this text is I am sure thinking, 'look there is no way there is such a vast conspiracy possible as this kind of Communist resurgence'. And it would be difficult to persuade people of it in these few paragraphs, but it might be possible to address a few obvious objections.

Objection 1: How could globalists corrupt so many people to bring this about?

Is it really possible that all of those countries worldwide could fall under the spell of a few corrupt globalists or Communists, it would have to involve the corruption of huge numbers of politicians and officials etc all over the world?

But would it, it might be interesting to ponder here these words from one of the globalists favourite philosophers (along with others like H. G. Wells, Aldous Huxley and Henry Kissinger), that has been floating around as a meme during the pandemic. The writer is Bertrand Russell:

> "It is to be expected that advances in physiology and psychology will give governments much more control over individual mentality than they now have even in totalitarian countries. Fichte laid it down that education should aim at destroying free-will, so that, after pupils have left school, they shall be incapable, throughout the rest of their lives, of thinking or acting otherwise than as their schoolmasters would have wished. But in his day this was an unattainable ideal: what he regarded as the best system in existence produced Karl Marx. In future such failures are not likely to occur where there is dictatorship. Diet, injections, and injunctions will combine, for a very early age, to

produce the sort of character and the sort of beliefs that the authorities consider desirable, and any serious criticism of the powers that be will become psychologically impossible. Even if all are miserable, all will believe themselves happy, because the government will tell them that they are so." [1]

The fact is that modern day society contains many people in very senior positions who consider themselves as sort of robots implementing doctrine outlined to them by international institutions/academics/scientists or officials, as Russell prophesied above. They are products of an education system that prioritises absorption and regurgitation, not thinking for oneself. Hence its actually easy for a group of globalists to dominate societies and countries around the world, once they set the international 'best practice' rules or their version of 'the established science' then 'leaders', academics and scientists around the word will follow them blindly.

This has been noticed by experts on this crisis, like Dr Andrew Kaufman M.D.:

> "The more broader aspect of this is that we are taught to get our information from experts, designated experts and authority figures, right.
>
> In school, in compulsory schooling, they tell us what the truth is. They don't have, there is no inquiry, there is no discovery, there is no research, right. There is no critical analysis, its pretty much being told information and then you are said to be smart if you memorise that information and you regurgitate it back but there is nothing around critical thinking.
>
> And so we have now basically like a population of adults without critical thinking skills and without the wherewithal to question things and to understand what dogma is, so that they can uncover it and not necessarily, you know, follow along and make decisions based upon it.
>
> But its a real big uphill climb and, you know I

am not sure why some people are able to see things or not but when you are trying to interact or communicate with someone that's indoctrinated in that way and they are not aware of it you cannot have a rational discussion, like because they cannot like objectively consider information." [2]

All you need to do is direct the head of this 'scientific consensus', meaning the international bodies, and in the modern world to a remarkable degree the policies just cascade down from there, unchecked.

Objection 2: Has any senior worldwide politician or figure agreed with this analysis?

Would not some honest figure see through all this and warn us? But indeed there are some serious figures that somewhat anyway endorse this view of the pandemic, and lots of other straws in the wind, including curious documents that point this way. For example consider here Archbishop Carlo Maria Vigano, formerly the number three man in running the Vatican, after the Pope and the Secretary of State, and later the Papal ambassador to the United States, who in this letter, signed as well by Cardinals Muller, Zen and Pujats, is sympathetic to this 'conspiracy theory' view of the exploitation of the pandemic:

> "The criminalization of personal and social relationships must likewise be judged as an unacceptable part of the plan of those who advocate isolating individuals in order to better manipulate and control them.
>
> ...
>
> We have reason to believe, on the basis of official data on the incidence of the epidemic as related to the number of deaths, that there are powers interested in creating panic among the world's population with the sole aim of permanently imposing unacceptable forms of restriction on freedoms, of controlling people and

of tracking their movements. The imposition of these illiberal measures is a disturbing prelude to the realization of a world government beyond all control.

...

We are fighting against an invisible enemy that seeks to divide citizens, to separate children from their parents, grandchildren from their grandparents, the faithful from their pastors, students from teachers, and customers from vendors. Let us not allow centuries of Christian civilization to be erased under the pretext of a virus, and an odious technological tyranny to be established, in which nameless and faceless people can decide the fate of the world by confining us to a virtual reality." [3]

Archbishop Vigano also wrote:

"We will probably find that in this colossal operation of social engineering there are people who have decided the fate of humanity, arrogating to themselves the right to act against the will of citizens and their representatives in the governments of nations.

We will also discover that the riots in these days were provoked by those who, seeing that the virus is inevitably fading and that the social alarm of the pandemic is waning, necessarily have had to provoke civil disturbances, because they would be followed by repression which, although legitimate, could be condemned as an unjustified aggression against the population. The same thing is also happening in Europe, in perfect synchrony...It will not be surprising if, in a few months, we learn once again that hidden behind these acts of vandalism and violence there are those who hope to profit from the dissolution of the social order so as to build a world without freedom: Solve et Coagula, as the Masonic adage teaches." [4]

Objection 3: At the end of the day we just don't live in that kind of Orwellian era, we have a multi-party, wide franchise, democracy for example

Under the Communist system oftentimes you get multiparty elections and voting systems but of course all parties in practice conform to the will of the state. Also historically many Communist countries were subservient to international institutions, like the Warsaw Pact or the dominance of Russia or China, and couldn't pass laws contrary to these supranational or international institutions.

Obviously in Ireland we have very little say over the laws passed in recent times, they are generally imposed on us by the EU. And as regards political parties, on all major issues (e.g. membership of the EU and Brexit, mass immigration, climate change, abortion and other anti-Catholic Church debates) they are absolutely entirely in lockstep together, just like in, other, Communist countries. There is no such thing as an Irish political party of any size disagreeing on these, the major issues in Ireland. No national, or even local, parliamentarian in anyway objected to the house arrests and the butchering of Irish people's right to travel outside their homes, to work, to assemble or go to Church worship.

Hence it really isn't a functioning democracy, you cannot in reality vote for a party with a practical chance of getting elected who will in any meaningful way change the administration of the country.

Objection 4: Our freedoms are protected by a written constitution backed up by independent courts

So what about the constitution? Don't we have a free and democratic society guaranteed in this country by that constitution, irrespective of what TDs and Senators think or do? Well it certainly says so in the constitution but no organ of the state or member of the legal profession – with the exception of Tracey O'Mahoney – made any objection when these rights were destroyed by the recent Covid-19 legislation (right to work is article 45.2.i, assemble 40.6.1.ii and freedom to practice ones religion 44.2.1). When two distinguished journalists tried to challenge this in the courts, at a cost of €50,000, the High Court would not even allow a hearing because, in it's opinion, stating that any of these rights had been infringed turns out to be 'not arguable' in an Irish court. This is such an astonishing statement, when obviously the state had just destroyed these rights guaranteed by the constitution, that you would have to agree with the two journalists verdict on it, Gemma O'Doherty:

> "There has been an effective coup by an unelected government, a government firmly rejected by the Irish people." [5]

John Waters:

> "I say to you we are finished, our country is finished, our Republic is finished, our democracy is finished, the rule of law is finished in this society, in this country, if we do not get, if we do not win this action that would mean that the constitution has been suspended." [6]

Objection 5: We are protected from such state oppression by a free and independent media

In Communist societies of course the media are just another arm of the state, reinforcing whatever propaganda line is being put out but also, famously in many Communist countries, sometimes hyping up minor differences within the ruling elite or between the controlled political parties, in order to create the illusion of democracy and a free press.

Right now the government has virtually taken over the small islands of the media it did not previously control, moving in to directly fund local radio for example,[7] now that advertisements from the independent business sector have collapsed. This has given rise to a society where the citizenry are virtually brainwashed into believing the latest propaganda by the state.

You think brainwashing is too strong? In Ireland right now you can not listen/watch/or read any organ of the media without:

– on radio, repeated spoken advertisements from the 'government of Ireland' advising people to 'stay at home', reinforcing the house arrest message;

– on television, very widely hyped press conferences stating the same thing, with again the reinforcing repetitive advertisements, including printed on podia when government spokespeople are speaking, also the message 'stay at home', and its successor messages, placed permanently at the corner of the TV screen throughout all its programming;

– in newspapers, massive prominent advertisements paid by the state, and sometimes by multinationals, saying the same thing;

– on the internet: facebook, twitter and youtube, and all Irish web fora known to this writer, have nearly half the page of the initial screen devoted to advertising the government's propaganda here;

– the familiar government yellow Covid-19 posters are everywhere on the public streets, in particular marked out on the pavements, shops and Churches etc, even wild beauty spots are frequently closed off, still, with those advertisements and posters;

– all letters and parcels received in Ireland are stamped with 'Stay at Home/HSE.ie', again so that people will support the house arrests and love their jailers.

Actually I think the most extreme film you have ever seen of 1984 style state propaganda has not come close to the type of society we are in right now.

Footnotes
1. Bertrand Russell, *The Impact of Science on Society* (Bombay, 1944), p.92.

2. https://www.youtube.com/watch?v=TgVdjAgg2J0 48:47.

3.   https://www.lifesitenews.com/news/four-cardinals-join-global-appeal-decrying-crackdown-on-basic-freedoms-over-coronavirus .

4.   https://www.lifesitenews.com/opinion/archbishop-viganos-powerful-letter-to-president-trump-eternal-struggle-between-good-and-evil-playing-out-right-now .

This is by an anonymous, but long running and well known, Australian Satanist called Aloysius Fozdyke commenting on the current situation which he says he helped bring about:
> "Have you noticed how the sheeple love all the new rules? It's based on the 3Ds program of debility, dependency, and dread.
>
> We're using isolation (quarantine, social distancing, and church closing), perception (think MSM), threats (you must get tested, have the vaccine and download the app), degradation (science denier and being non-essential), the enforcement of trivial demands (to develop compliance) and the occasional indulgence (to demonstrate our omnipotence and omniscience)."
>
> (https://www.henrymakow.com/2020/07/insider-human-enslavement-according-to-plan.html .)

Another interesting document comes from 2010 and is said to refer to a Masonic meeting in London in 2005, described here by Bill Ryan of the Avalon Project:
> "The other thing that is being set up for this, and many people watching this will be aware that this is being set up in the background. We have a lot of information about this from a number of good researchers from many countries who are reporting this on the internet. That things are being set up in many of the Western countries for there to be heavy controls over populations: martial law, increased powers on security forces who are not just the army or the police.
>
> ...
>
> And in this rollout of this crazy scenario, where it is intended that there will be a limited nuclear exchange in the Middle East, the idea is that, as the world looks upon this with horror, then they will demand from their governments that there are heavy controls over travel, over communication, over people who meet, over people who protest in the streets. They want to make sure that they don't

have crazy bombers on air planes, crazy bombers in the shopping malls, they want to make sure – and because people will be driven into fear by this – they'll request and demand and insist on heavy controls from their governments, which will be justified. And this is where you will kind of get the martial law situation in all the Western countries. It is intended as a justification.

...

And then the next thing that happens, in this chess game that is being played, is that biological weapons are released on China. He heard this being discussed in this meeting. They will release a flu-like virus that will be genetically targeted against the Chinese population. It's racially targeted against the Chinese people. It's designed to spread like wildfire and to knock out a large number of the Chinese people. And these people in this meeting were laughing about this. They said: 'China will catch a cold'. Those were their words: 'China will catch a cold'. And they were laughing about the fact that these biological weapons will wreak havoc among the Chinese population.

After that, then what effectively will be a kind of plague will actually spread right across the world to the West as well. Our source was not clear whether this was a Chinese retaliation, or whether the thing would just spread out of control, in the way that it would be very understandable if it did, whether it's racially targeted or not. These things actually mutate.

So now you've got a situation where there's been a limited nuclear war in the Middle East; there's a pandemic that really is sweeping across the world and really is killing people, very visibly, and you've got this totalitarian military lockdown in all the governments in the Western world, because everyone is going to be in panic about all of this."
(https://www.youtube.com/watch?v=JlP2tqITxWE 2:41, 3:58 and 5:28. As with all these links, this author does not endorse the Avalon Project, and in fact would be very sceptical of a lot of their thinking.)

Incidentally it would be a mistake to think that powerful people had not planned for a pandemic such as this long since, and had already put in place their procedures to deal with it. *Event201*, which predicted a worldwide Coronavirus pandemic in a videotaped simulation on the 18th October 2019, is by now a well known example: https://www.youtube.com/watch?v=Vm1-DnxRiPM , but it was preceded the previous year by the much less well known *Clade X* simulation using much the same personalities: https://www.youtube.com/watch?v=sJ1x8SlNxj0 .

Another one of these pandemic planning type scenarios was prepared by the Rockefeller Foundation and the Global Business Network in May 2010, called *Scenarios for the Future of Technology and International Development* it describes a future pandemic scenario under the chapter *lockstep*, from which:

> "The United States's initial policy of "strongly discouraging" citizens from flying proved deadly in its leniency, accelerating the spread of the virus not just within the U.S. but across borders. However, a few countries did fare better — China in particular. The Chinese government's quick imposition and enforcement of mandatory quarantine for all citizens, as well as its instant and near-hermetic sealing off of all borders, saved millions of lives, stopping the spread of the virus far earlier than in other countries and enabling a swifter post-pandemic recovery."
>
> (https://archive.org/details/pdfy-tNG7MjZUicS-wiJb/mode/2up .)

A further example of this is a 2007 planning exercise in the banking sector involving people like Stephen R. Malphrus, staff director for management at the Federal Reserve Board:

> "The new guidance was a result of information learned from running a simulated pandemic exercise in the fall of 2007 involving more than 2,775 organizations, of which 62% were banks and credit unions with securities firms, insurance companies, and government agencies comprising the remainder. This exercise was sponsored jointly by the U.S. Treasury and the Securities Industry and Financial Markets Association. The exercise was conducted by the Financial and Banking Information Infrastructure Committee (FBIIC) and the Financial Services Sector Coordinating Council (FSSCC).
>
> ...
>
> Malphrus also cites the "doctrine of social isolation" indicating health authorities would recommend public assemblies be limited. Understanding state and local policies will be critical to any successful plan. "Work with local health and safety authorities," says Malphrus and "understand their plans for school closings, quarantines, and isolation."
>
> ...
>
> "If the board is attempting to prioritize its activities, it should first ask: 'Who was working over the Thanksgiving holidays?' That will give good insight into what is absolutely necessary to run the business in survival mode. In other words, treat the disruption as a prolonged holiday.
>
> ...
>
> The guidance issued by regulators cautions that even the

best preparations for telecommuting could encounter problems in the event of a pandemic. Specifically, it warns that increased use of the Internet by at-home workers and bored Web stay-at-homes would likely reduce residential service Internet speeds by 50%.

In addition to raising concerns about performance problems for telecommuters, the report reconsiders the importance of telecommuting's role during a pandemic.

...

And beyond that? "It wouldn't hurt to include a plan for dealing with a second wave," adds Monroe."
(https://www.godlikeproductions.com/forum1/message9079 05/pg1 .)

Another issue that we can be clear about, is that the powers that be during the pandemic knew very well the effect of the fear they generated and have been quietly using the pandemic to reset society according to their wishes, at least in the UK. Here a few quotes from an internal document from the behavioural sciences sub-group of the all powerful UK Scientific Advisory Group for Emergencies (SAGE) of the 22nd March 2020, leaked to the *UK Column News* channel:

"Use the media to increase the sense of personal threat...A substantial number of people still do not feel personally threatened...The perceived level of personal threat needs to be increased among those who are complacent..."
(https://www.youtube.com/watch?v=tVLq0h2t-rk .)

UK Column also heard from a senior UK Government/Civil Service figure who said they internally discussed how:

"Covid19 [Lockdown] is an extraordinary opportunity NOT to re-open 50/60% of what each company does...schools, care homes, coal fired power stations...they are garbage, they are toxic...you just DON'T RE-OPEN them – ever...'Re-Invent' society because we will never get this opportunity again in our lifetime."
(Ibid.)

Finally another curious document that people might like to consider is the Toronto Protocols, what is stated to be notes from two meetings of globalists, one in 1967 and the next in 1985 both in Toronto in Canada but of global significance, a few extracts from this:

"So then we can inaugurate what was announced by both our past creations: "The communist system who prophesied a world revolution set in motion by all the rejects of the earth", and "Nazism in which we had announced a New World Order for 1000 years". That is our ultimate goal, the award of the work of all the brave fallen for the performance of this work over the centuries. Say it loud and clear: "All the Brothers of the past Lodges, who died in anonymity for the realization of this ideal that we are now able to touch with the tips of our fingers."

It is generally acknowledged that Man, once having secured his basic needs (food, clothing and shelter), is much more likely to be less vigilant. Let us allow him to lull his conscience, while we direct our own thing in his mind ["tout en orientant à notre guise son esprit en lui créant"], by creating favourable economic conditions. So, during this period of the 70s where our agents will slip across the different spheres of Society to accept our new standards in Education, Legal Rights, and Social Policy, we will spread it around in a confident economic climate.

Work for all; the opening of Credit for all; Recreation for all, will work in tandem to create an illusion of a new social class: the "Middle Class". Because once we have achieved our goals, this "class" in the middle, between the secular poor, and us rich, will definitely disappear by cutting off all means of survival.

...

Thus it will be possible to increase dramatically the burden on the State by multiplying, without any limits, the mass of intellectual-functionaries [employed by the state]. Insured, for years in advance, with material security, they are therefore perfect performers of the "Governmental Authority", in other words, our "Power."

Creating an impressive mass of public servants who, alone, will form a Government in the government, regardless of which political party will be in power. This machine can anonymously one day serve as a lever, when the time comes, to accelerate the economic collapse of nation states, because they can not indefinitely sustain such a payroll without having to incur debts beyond their means.

On the other hand, this same machine that will give an image of cold and unresponsive government; this complex machine, useless in many of its functions, will serve as a cover and protection against the people. For who will dare to venture through the mazes of this labyrinth to assert his personal grievances?

...

The constant influx of "Electronic Technology" will make sure all the means to file, identify, and monitor all individuals in populations of the West. For those who do not represent "Exploitable Profitability" by ourselves, we will ensure they are eliminated through all the local civil wars that we have taken care to break out here and there through: the work of our servants; and the "Fall of the Economy" of the Nation-States; and the "Oppositions and Claims" of various groups within those states.

...

2. – Encourage "Student Causes" for all cases related to the "Ecology". The mandatory protection of the latter will be a major asset on the day we will have pushed the Nation-States to exchange their "Domestic Debt" for a loss of 33% of all their territories remaining in the wild.

3. – Let us fill the inner void of that youth by initiating, from a very young age, the world of computers. Use this as its education system. A slave in the service of another slave we control.

...

5. – To ensure at all costs the success of such an endeavour, let us ensure that our agents, who have infiltrated the Ministries of Intergovernmental Affairs and Immigration of the Nation-States, make major changes to the Statutes of these ministries. These changes will essentially open the doors of immigration to Western countries with a large mass of immigrants entering across their frontiers (immigration that we have indeed caused by having taken care to break out here and there, new localised conflicts). Through well-orchestrated press campaigns targeting public opinion in the Nation-States, we provoke them to accept a large influx of refugees which will have the effect of destabilizing the domestic economy, and increasing racial tensions, in their territory. We will ensure that groups of foreign extremists are part of the influx of immigrants, which will facilitate the political, economic, and social, destabilization of the Nations concerned.

...

22 . – The emergence of the next global commitment to a "Multi-National Military Force" will go hand in hand with the establishment, within the United Nations, of an "Multi-Jurisdictional Intervention Force". Using this combination of "Effective Police and Military", created by the same pretext of increasing political and social instability within these states collapsing under the burden of economic problems, we can better control the western populations. Here, the excessive use of electronic filing and identification of individuals will provide a complete monitoring of all populations."

This is just a taste of the numerous documents and leaks out there that surely the general public should now engage with and take seriously? For the reason why I will leave you with the ending words of Serge Monast as he first published this document:

> "So, the "PROTOCOL OF TORONTO (6.6.6.)", myth or reality?
>
> It is for you to answer...
>
> For you to see in the recent past and future events, if these "documents" belong to the realm of fiction or reality.
>
> For you to realize that fear has no other purpose than to paralyse you and put you to thank those who want to control you, to better enslave you according to their interests, which are ultimately, not yours."
>
> (*The Toronto Protocol: The real plan of the Global Elite?* (Corstown, 2012), p.14-15, 19-20, 24-25, 28-29. There is also a video discussion of these protocols here: https://www.altcensored.com/watch?v=-oth1vS2xR0 , and further information on Serge Monast is available here: https://heartofeuropeblog.blogspot.com/2015/11/toronto-protocols-revealed-20-years-ago.html .)

5. RTE1 *Prime Time*, Thursday 25/6/2020, https://www.rte.ie/player/series/prime-time/SI0000000825?epguid=IH000382998 , 26:26.

6. Ibid.

7.   https://www.agriland.ie/farming-news/e2-5-million-funding-available-for-local-and-independent-radio/ . And newspapers:

> "The Department of the Taoiseach told the Sunday Times recently that the government was directing advertising to newspapers to support them.
>
> ...
>
> By some reckonings, the government of Ireland today is one of the biggest advertisers in the country. And with so many others currently out of the market, its importance will only have increased.
>
> Meanwhile, following years and years of decline, many newspapers were already fairly desperate. After this latest blow, many are now fighting for their very survival.
>
> It is clear who holds the power in this relationship."
>
> (https://www.dublininquirer.com/2020/05/13/sam-the-dangers-of-using-government-advertising-to-prop-up-suffering-newspapers .)

CONCLUSION

Yes of course it is a remarkable statement to say that we are now living in Communist times, but its just true. Sure it is different in many ways to what it was like in Eastern Europe in the 20th century, but nonetheless the same policies we can see in force in our own times now.

The bad news is that if we are in such a State then we have much more to look forward to. State bankruptcy, for example, is always on the agenda of a Communist country because their doctrine is all about spending money and not how to generate it. Food supply issues, even starvation, are another frequent theme of a Communist State, because the elaborate supply chains and the skills of farming and food production are particularly incompatible with the top down economic planning of these type of States.

How we got here I guess is a theme for another day, but at least if we recognise we are here then maybe it might shake the complacency of the general public to at least try and take the country back from our EU and international masters.

We can only hope, because, I again respectfully submit, on this our time is rapidly running out.

If you liked this book you might like to read some of the author's other works, including:

A Guide to the 18th century land records in the Irish Registry of Deeds
The Registry of Deeds in Dublin contains a vast repository of summaries of Irish land transactions for the 18th century. This collection is particularly important, to genealogists among others, because of the destruction of other historical records in Ireland for the same period, especially since the Four Courts fire of 1922. In this guide you will find a description of the records held there, an explanation of the different Irish land and currency units used, and a wide ranging discussion of Irish land transactions and registries of the period and somewhat later. This includes the influence of the Penal Laws, the nature of Irish marriage settlements and the economic climate and prices prevailing in Ireland in that century.
978-0-9556812-9-5

An Creideaṁ
This book seeks to illustrate the type of literature that shaped and influenced the Irish people's faith over the centuries. It is intended as a cornucopia of Catholic writing, a skirl around the kind of books and journals that graced Irish priest's libraries over the years. Outlined in chronological order it gives the full text of the Confession of St. Patrick, the Life of St. Columbanus, an ancient Irish tract on the mass; extracts from the Confessions of St. Augustine, the Irish Annals, and the fiction of Canon Sheehan; some theology from St. Thomas Aquinas, from 'A Handbook of Moral Theology', and the doctrine of Purgatory from an old Maynooth theologian; historical or contemporary accounts from all centuries, all the way from Tertullian, through Lough Derg in the 15th century, the Cromwellian Wars of the 17th century, to the social and economic teachings of the Church in the 19th and early 20th centuries.
978-0-9556812-3-3

Slí na Fírinne
This English language book puts the traditional Catholic proofs of God's existence into a modern context. It covers most of the arguments raging in the theism v atheism debate and also includes quotes on the nature of God and his existence from c.80 philosophers and scientists.
978-0-9556812-8-8

Shakespeare was Irish!
As more and more scholars come to realise that the accepted story of William Shakespeare is untenable, this book tries to unmask the covert Irish influence on his work and the remarkable career of William Nugent, the only Irish candidate ever put forward for Shakespeare. It includes the full text of many original documents on Irish history, from the Reformation to the 1641 Rebellion.
978-0-9556812-1-9